IN DUE TIME

9 PRACTICAL HABITS TO ACHIEVING SUCCESS

MOSES JOHNSON, PT, DPT

Author: Moses Johnson
© Prosperous Roots LLC

No part of this book may be reproduced, stored in a retrieval system, or transmitted in any form or by any means, electronic, mechanical, photocopying, recording, or otherwise, without the prior written permission of the author, except as provided by the U.S.A. copyright law.

DEDICATION

I would like to dedicate this book to my mother, Ann Cobbs, my father, James "Vern" Johnson, to my close friends and family, as they often supported me in all of my endeavors, and in special honor of Mary Suggs, Shirley Nesmith, Lucy Vines and Shirley Johnson, the matriarchs of my family.

ABOUT THE AUTHOR

Moses Johnson is a first-generation graduate of Norfolk State University and Howard University, where he earned his bachelor's degree in Exercise Science/Kinesiotherapy and his doctorate degree in Physical Therapy. Born and raised in Richmond, Virginia's Northside Community, he is best known for his health advocacy and inspiring others in the face of challenging times. He is a member of many organizations, which include Partnership for The Future, Golden Key Honour Society, Phi Epsilon Kappa, RVA Fitness Warriors and The Shirley Johnson-Clarke Foundation. Undeterred from his previous failures, he has been a beacon of hope to others and exemplifies how they can overcome adversity. His book, *In Due Time,* serves to instruct readers with practical routines/habits to achieve success.

ACKNOWLEDGEMENT

My advice to you is that you keep your faith and continue to work diligently towards your goals, even when you cannot see the progress of your hard work.

"Delayed does not mean denied" – as my mother would say.

One must comprehend the principles of success before putting them into practice. The goal of this book is to show how the principles of success may be applied to all of our aspirations and goals in life rather than to outline and explain in detail what they are.

You are capable of becoming and doing anything in life! Your achievements, grandeur, and potential are entirely up to you, and you already possess all the qualities needed to realize your aspirations.

That is why I want you to read this quote several times:

"There is no such thing as a successful job; the successful job belongs to the man who owns it." And you are in control of your own destiny, whatever it is you want to become in life.

Our success and potential are something we create, grow, and decide for ourselves; it is not something outside of us that is dictated by our skills, knowledge, wealth, race, gender, or even environment.

Only when we comprehend and put into practice the fundamental rules and secrets for success will we be able to realize our aspirations and goals.

The success formula or secret that I've provided above is explored in more detail below. It is not at all a secret because all the great thinkers, artists, religious figures, generals, and politicians throughout history have recognized and applied these laws of success.

The success and development of today's top sports, entertainers, businesspeople, scientists, and politicians can be revealed and explained by the same concepts.

These laws are straightforward in theory but tremendously challenging in practice. Unreasonably assuming that the 'how-to' guidance from books, seminars, and even mentors will reveal and teach them the necessary information and intricacies of how to be successful, people far too frequently fail to recognize the fundamental simplicity of these qualities and behaviors. Even still, merely comprehending and believing in these ideas is insufficient; success and the fulfillment of aspirations can only be attained by the application of these ideas on a consistent basis.

I think everyone, regardless of color, religion, creed, or nation, can succeed if they follow the guidelines in "In Due Time." I'm grateful to everyone who has and will buy this book, and I'm grateful to the author for letting me tell you about my success.

Below are a few of the concepts that will be thoroughly discussed.

TABLE OF CONTENTS

DEDICATION	I
ABOUT THE AUTHOR	III
ACKNOWLEDGEMENT	V
INTRODUCTION	11

PART 1

CHAPTER 1: Maintain a Good Reputation	15
CHAPTER 2: Pursue Your Passion	24
CHAPTER 3: Give 110% to Everything You Do	34
CHAPTER 4: Practice Self-Care	45
CHAPTER 5: Be Optimistic, But Be Realistic	58
CHAPTER 6: Collaborate: 2 Brains Are Better Than 1	70
CHAPTER 7: Know Your Worth	78
CHAPTER 8: Be Consistent	86
CHAPTER 9: Do Your Best	97

PART 2

CHAPTER 10: Developing Your Network	107
CHAPTER 11: Embrace Productivity	117
CHAPTER 12: Additional Masterpiece Principles	126
FINAL NOTE	135

INTRODUCTION

The purpose of this book is to highlight 9 practical routines/habits that are needed for people to be successful. The inspiration for writing this book comes from the trials and tribulations I've faced and overcome while pursuing my dreams.

This book is intended for anyone who is in need of guidance, whether it is in following their career path, falling in love, or trying to figure out what it is exactly that they want to do in life.

As a first-generation graduate with a doctorate degree in Physical Therapy, a passion for music, and an avid book reader, my hope for you is that you find some inspiration from this book and apply it in your daily life.

PART 1

"A good reputation is more valuable than money"

– PUBLILIUS SYRUS

CHAPTER 1

Maintain a Good Reputation

A good reputation is a worthy asset a person can have. It can open doors and create better opportunities while making building relationships and trust easier. A good reputation is more desirable than silver or gold because it can help you get more opportunities and be successful in life. Of course, money can't buy you everything, but a good reputation can go a long way. People with good reputations are respected and trusted, leading to better jobs, relationships, and opportunities.

On the other hand, money is a limited resource that can only buy so much. It's undoubtedly essential to have enough money to live comfortably, it will never be able to buy happiness or true love.

A good reputation, on the other hand, has the power to make a person's life infinitely richer. So, in the end, it's clear that a good reputation is far more valuable than money.

Often times our circumstances are impacted by our financial stability. Many Americans and people abroad aspire to have access to a nice car, home, or career, which is predicated upon wealth. Living in America, a country that thrives off capitalism, there is working culture that believes that "the harder you work, the more money you will make," and we as citizens have a tendency to "chase the bag" in hopes of improving our current living state. Although having money allows for possessions of material things and can aid in the relief of daily stressors, a good reputation is worth more than money.

Whether you are a janitor or CEO of a Fortune 500 company, your reputation will make room for things that money can't buy. An individual with traits that are deemed unworthy of business does not make them a great business partner merely because they have more money. The saying "all money isn't good money" is a testament that people with bad reputations are not good for business.

Moreover, a bad reputation hinders a person from fruitful relationships, whether it is in their career, spouse, or community organization. A person of integrity who honors their word and does right by people will often have a good reputation. Being known among colleagues and peers as someone who is reliable will open doors you wouldn't even imagine. Having a good heart in combination with consistency, will, and determination can grant access to rooms that money can't buy. Yes, rich individuals may have the funds to afford certain expenses, but if a rich person has a questionable reputation, what exactly will they gain?

Barack Obama, the 44th President and the first Black President of the United States of America, is another individual who is regarded as having a good reputation. Barack Obama occupied the white house from 2008 – 2016 and successfully was able to serve for 2 terms. In 2016, Barack Obama had an approval rating of 54%, which was the highest approval rating for a president since Bill Clinton in the year 2000 (57%). During his presidency, he was able to rescue the economy by putting a halt to a Recession that lasted from December 2007 to June 2009.

In 2010, he signed the Affordable Care Act, also known as "Obama Care," which helped to improve access to affordable health coverage for millions of citizens in the United States. In addition, he was able to end the war in Iraq, increase benefits for veterans, address climate change, and support child nutrition (with the help of Michelle Obama) by allocating $4.5 billion towards the improvement in nutrition for school lunch programs. To be the first to do anything is a difficult task. I'd imagine when Shirley Chisholm, a black congresswoman who ran for president in 1972, and Jesse Jackson, a black American political activist who ran for president in 1984 and 1988, faced many challenges. It takes courage to be publicly scrutinized in the public eye – especially for Black Americans wanting to obtain political power. Given Obama's success, it was something that Americans had never seen before.

As a country, to witness a Black man encounter racist backlash and slanderous media propaganda while fixing the problems of American Citizens was unprecedented. Barack Obama was able to maintain his position as commander in chief without a single incident or scandal. His ability to lead with professionalism and a good reputation amongst his peers, colleagues, and the nation is what allowed him to occupy the oval office for eight years.

IN DUE TIME

Let's look at Jay-Z for an example. Jay-Z is a hip-hop musician who was born and raised in Marcy projects of Brooklyn, New York. He started his music career in the mid-'80s and would eventually partner with two of his friends and begin his own record label, Rocafella records, in 1996. By the early 2000s, he had built a reputation of being a well-known rapper throughout the United States. It is obvious today that Jay-Z is a household name whenever we discuss rap and debate who is the best MC, but make no mistake that this success story didn't happen overnight. In order for any person to have a good reputation, they must commit to consistency. Jay-Z was consistently in the studio, consistently putting forth 110% in everything that he does (we will discuss this principle in a later chapter) and consistently finding new business ventures to expand his portfolio.

When someone demonstrates consistency, not only is it a reflection of their determination, but it also makes them trustworthy. Imagine if Jay-Z decided to come to his studio sessions late and didn't show up for set rehearsals for live performances; the likelihood of him being successful would be slim. It is the consistency in your day-to-day habits that forms your reputation. Once you are able to adopt good habits such as showing up on time, getting things done in a timely manner, and holding yourself accountable, the doors of opportunity will open. The things that you are passionate about will make room for money, which I will discuss next.

But first, let's briefly learn about something that is crucial to our trip before I go on to the stage of passion. You must put God &

Family First in whatever you do, and I termed it "God and Family." Knowing God and caring for your family can help you to understand that a good reputation is always worth more than any amount of money.

Whatever your aspirations and objectives, never lose sight of what real success in life entails. True success is found not in achieving the goal but rather in the person we develop while working towards it.

All other triumphs will be failures if, while pursuing our dream, we neglect to put God first and prioritize spending time with our families. In the end, it will be much simpler to deal with the disappointment that comes with some failures than it will be to deal with the disappointment that comes with some victories because they weren't the correct accomplishments. The 'real' triumphs of life will result from putting God and family first, but oddly, having these as your priority will also contribute to and be the reason for all other successes you achieve.

After all, let us glance through the chart and consider 3 actions that are associated with a good and bad reputation.

Things associated with good reputation

Things associated with bad reputation

☐ Meet deadlines

☐ Taking shortcuts

☐ Come up with ideas to improve something

☐ Only meeting expectations, instead of exceeding them

☐ Give credit to others

☐ Not trusting your gut instinct

Let's go on to the second point in this respect, where I mentioned I would discuss passion; as a rule, we might abide by it to accomplish our intended goals.

CHAPTER SUMMARY

- Your reputation will make room for things that money can't buy
- A bad reputation hinders a person from fruitful relationships
- The things that you are passionate about will make room for money

ACTION PLANS

1. As of now, I will maintain a good reputation to reach success.

2. As of now, I will _____

IN DUE TIME

"The best preparation for tomorrow is to do today's work superbly well and follow with passion."

— WILLIAM OSLER

CHAPTER 2

Pursue Your Passion

Being passionate about your profession is essential for success. One of the main characteristics that distinguish practically any highly successful individual from others is a passion for whatever it is that person does. That person will put forth whatever effort is necessary to flourish and be successful because they genuinely enjoy what they do.

As children, we all develop a passion for something, whether it is learning to play an instrument, a sport, or fine art. Often, many people grow up and become accustomed to the ways of the world rather than pursue their dreams. Part of this can be due to a lack of ambition, guidance, or in the worst case, falling on hard times. Despite whatever setbacks you may face in life, pursuing your dreams can be empowering. Some may wonder, what is it that they are passionate about, and that can be answered with one question: what is it that you would do for free? In my life, I've had to work countless intern hours that I wasn't being paid for. To be able to get up, get dressed, and dedicate 8 hours a day for

Pursue Your Passion

5 days a week for free is a sacrifice I've made in pursuit of my dreams. For the company, I was providing extra labor. For me, I was gaining experience and exposure in a career that I was passionate about. At times I was tired but knowing that I could make a difference in people's lives every single day with the decision to be present was enough motivation for me. In those moments, I wasn't paid, but my passion is what made work feel like a hobby. There's a saying that 'if you follow your passion, you'll never work a day in your life". Don't be afraid to pursue a career that doesn't pay as much. If it is something that you are passionate about, opportunities to make more money will come.

Let's say, for example, that you are passionate about cooking. When you are alone, baking, frying, and sauteing food is something you find of interest. During family gatherings, you look forward to making your favorite dishes to serve your loved ones. Not only does cooking satisfy your hunger, but the process in itself of making something from scratch that everyone enjoys makes you feel good internally. You receive compliments about your cooking style, and this fuels you to continue to cook food. Money isn't a motive for you, and you love to see people's reactions. Your family raves about your cooking to their neighbors, and now everyone wants a slice of what you have. If you were to start a restaurant business today, you'd likely have a handful of customers. The passion which you put into your craft is tasty, and everyone can tell that you take pride in cooking. Because of this, people are willing to pay for your services. You have a reputation for great service, and everyone looks forward to your meal preparation stories. Many will try to replicate your recipe, but you are the one with the Midas touch. You've mastered the culinary arts, and because of your reputable service, people are willing to pay you for your meals. When you are passionate, people will notice, and you'll live a life with no regrets because, unlike some, you decided to pursue your dreams.

Having a strong sense of desire comes from having a strong sense of passion. Your desire will motivate you to keep pursuing your interests despite any challenges.

All successes and accomplishments in life begin fundamentally with a burning desire to realize a goal or ideal. But do not be misled; desire is not the same as expectation, wish, or interest. Desire is the same as motivation, dedication, determination, and the readiness to go above and beyond to achieve the desired outcome.

Your passion and desire for something will also serve as a guide for your ability to "Think Big," "Dream Big," and "Think Differently."

You might want something, but are you genuinely working toward a dream or a goal? Do you succumb to the prevailing mediocrity culture and feel constrained by your circumstances, or do you genuinely dream big and think large? You will continue to be ordinary unless you do.

Think large if you want to be huge because we really are what we think.

And know that you are in bad company if you find yourself speaking, acting, and thinking like the majority (in terms of desires, objectives, and "success" in life).

Dream boldly. Dare to think and act differently. And always think broadly. Then, with sufficient mental conditioning, belief, and consistent activity, your lofty goals and large ideas will be translated into deeds that ultimately result in enormous accomplishments.

Since dreams are one of the cornerstones of achievement, they rank among the most important success concepts. Success is practically impossible without a dream. A dream is something you see or experience in your head that is different from what you see or experience right now, or that cannot be found when you are dreaming, according to an understandable definition. For instance, The Wright Brothers fantasized about owning an airplane because such a thing did not exist in their day.

Because your dream is your success, having a dream is like starting your search for achievement. What do you dream about? It need not be as outrageous as the Wright Brothers, but it should still be worthwhile to pursue.

Remembering what you wished you might be or had as a child is the finest strategy to look for your goal. Because you were unaware of or unconcerned with reality when you were young, your ideal was inspiring and expansive. As you get older, though, your ideal might have changed as you begin to internalize the idea of the impossible. Take some time to reflect on your past thoughts or to do a soul-searching exercise.

Dreams live on; you will reclaim them. A burning dream is far superior to simply having a dream. People who have turned their lives around 360 degrees may exhibit burning dreams. A man who has experienced poverty has a lofty aspiration to enjoy a life of luxury. A horrible child typically harbors a deep desire to please their parents.

Money will follow if you have huge dreams regarding your interest. 95 percent of Americans experience financial hardship. They work to make a life and eke out an existence. Their jobs are not enjoyable. They are not really passionate about their line of work.

What a pity. Financial success is fueled by passion. You will never become truly wealthy if you don't have passion for what you do.

Why?

Why do the majority of Americans live such desperate lives?

The solution is not particularly difficult. Most people never decide on or come up with a primary goal they want to pursue in life. Most people never learn how to establish their key aim or articulate their major purpose. You are rudderless if you don't have a significant life objective. You don't have a strategy for success. You cannot aspire to reach your limitless potential without a strategy or a road map for reaching a significant objective.

But have courage. Never let it be too late.

There is always time because so many people today are living well into their seventies.

How do you decide what your main life goal is? The solution is to have passion. To discover what you are actually passionate about, you must look within.

Enthusiasm is a gauge of passion. Find the cause, the reason, and the aim that you are passionate about. What energizes you, and how do you know?

When you are engaged in an activity that brings you a lot of delight, you can tell if you are enthusiastic, especially when the action is carried out without reference to a clock. When time goes by quickly, you are getting close.

When you pursue a purpose or goal without considering the time required, you are doing something you genuinely enjoy. You know you're on the right track when working doesn't feel like an effort. The top 5% of earnings in America who are wealthy claim to never feel like they are working. They enjoy what they do, and as the day comes to an end, they eagerly anticipate tomorrow. The following morning, they do not complain about the labor that is waiting for them. You must determine your main mission in life if you want to do anything significant in life.

Be perfect, at least in your actions. Even while there is no such thing as a perfect man, you can at least perform the tasks you are familiar with to the point where others will deem them to be flawless.

Let's move on to the next rule!

CHAPTER SUMMARY

- Pursuing your dreams can be empowering
- Don't be afraid to pursue a career that doesn't pay as much if it is something that you are passionate about
- When you are passionate, people will notice, and you'll live a life with no regrets

ACTION PLANS

1. As of now, I will seek the counsel of the wise who can help me reach my goals in due time.

2. As of now, I will _____

_____

_____

_____

_____

_____

_____

_____

_____

_____

_____

_____

_____

IN DUE TIME

"What you lack in talent can be made up with desire, hustle and giving 110% all the time

— DON ZIMMER

CHAPTER 3

Give 110% to Everything You Do

When you decide to work your first gig, play professional sports, or entertain a relationship with a significant other, the determining factor for your success will primarily rely upon effort. You can be the smartest person with the highest IQ in your class, but if you don't put forth the effort, you will not reap the reward. You can be the most talented or skilled individual in your game of choice, but that alone does not make you the best. In most cases, you don't have to be a genius to be successful, but you will have to put forth 110% in everything that you do. Giannis Antetokounmpo, a power forward for the Milwaukee Bucks, won his first championship ring and was voted the finals MVP in the 2021 NBA finals. He couldn't shoot like a Kevin Durant, Drive to the rim like a Lebron James, nor is he as talented as Stephen Curry, but one thing he does give every play is 110% effort. During that same NBA finals, he suffered structural damage after hyperextending his knee in Game 4. This is not to say that you should receive injury when accomplishing a task. However, this is to highlight the commendable effort to return to play and dominate an entire series, scoring 50 points in game 6 to win a franchise its second ring in history. So whether you decide to become an aspiring artist, teacher, ball player, etc., it is best that you do it with 110% effort.

In order to give 110% to something, you must know what should be prioritized. Having this understanding will help you to understand where to concentrate your effort. Let's say, for example, that you want to start a business. You hate your current job situation and that you dread having to come to work on Monday mornings. If starting a business is important to you, first, you would need to think about what it is that you're good at. Would you want to start a for-profit or a non-profit organization? The more specific that you can get into detailing your business, the more the likelihood that it is to come to fruition. Once you are able to describe the work you want to do, next, you should identify your strengths and weaknesses, opportunities, and threats. This is known as the *SWOT analysis*. This will help to prioritize where you should concentrate your efforts. Like most people, we all have dreams and aspirations. The difference between a dream remaining accumulated thoughts and obtaining them is the actionable strategies in which we put forth. Like Giannis and his teammates running to the NBA finals, there is a strategy that is needed when facing your competition. There is a strategy in how you are preparing for a game. There is a strategy in just about everything – from the marketing of goods to the arrangement layout of buildings, parks, and monuments. The most important thing that you can do is to concentrate your energy by giving 110% to everything that you are dedicated to becoming. Your daily routine becomes a reflection of you. You must develop discipline because you won't always be inspired.

Maggie Lena Walker, an African American businesswoman and civil rights trailblazer, personifies the meaning of giving 110% effort. Born to enslaved parents on July 15, 1864, in Richmond, Virginia, Walker was able to overcome social, political, and economic barriers to advance the African American Community. In 1903, she founded the St. Luke Penny Savings Bank and became the first woman in the history of the United States to charter a bank. Walker's effort is what made Richmond the epicenter of black finance and the birthplace of America's Black Wall Street. In 1920, Walker was able to issue more than 600 mortgages to members of the African Americans Community, making homeownership a reality. In 1924, the St. Luke Penny Savings Bank had spread across Virginia, opening 1,500 branches and providing service to more than 50,000 members. Many other banks failed during the Great Depression, which took place between 1929-1939, but St. Luke Penny Savings Bank was able to stand the test of time. Prior to the banking business, Walker was an entrepreneur at heart. Within her lifetime, she assisted her mom, who worked as a laundress, became a schoolteacher, the head of an insurance company, owned a department store, worked as a newspaper editor, and published the newspaper for St. Luke Herald. She was a member of many organizations, including the Independent Order of St. Luke National Association of Colored Women (NACW), and served as the vice president of the National Association for the Advancement of

Colored People (NAACP) in Richmond. It is true that Maggie L. Walker was responsible for many roles, and because of her efforts to put 110% into everything that she did, she was able to bring a source of pride to the African American Community in Richmond. She wasn't a woman who inherited a fortune, but her impact is worth millions.

Believing in yourself and that your dreams are attainable are among the other things you should take care of because doing so may enable you to accomplish anything you set out to do with at least 110 percent accuracy.

You must realize that anything is possible for us to become and to do! But unless someone had faith and trust that the concept, objective, or ambition was achievable, nothing truly remarkable had ever been done. Each of us spends too much time dwelling on things that are truly just in our heads, such as our own shortcomings and failures, our lack of skills or resources, our worries and doubts, the skills and talents of others, or our own limitations.

Actually, it's our potential that scares us, and most of the time, mediocrity and being average is attractive because they excuse us from having to put in the effort required to be successful. Truthfully, a lack of self-confidence is the root of the issue and the main reason why the majority of individuals don't realize their potential, objectives, and dreams in life.

This is one of the causes why we must silence the voices of fear and skepticism unless we choose not to offer the world everything we have at 110%.

Remember that the world expects nothing less than the best from you, so you should silence the voice inside of you that inspires doubt and dread.

You must realize that the only constraints in life are those we imagine, nurture, and maintain in our own imaginations. Though everyone has brilliant ideas, attainable goals, and limitless potential, they never act on them because they spend too much time listening to voices of failure, fear, and doubt. Fear and uncertainty are unneeded worries and signs of low confidence. They reveal one's lack of mental discipline and are the root cause of the majority of failures. Ironically, everyone experiences these universal feelings of fear and doubt, which lead to inertia and delay. Thankfully, anybody can manage and get over fear and uncertainty, but doing so takes persistent daily work because these voices never go away.

We must continually control our thinking and purge terms like "can't," "quit," "unable," "impossible," etc., from our language. To live our dreams, we must overcome our doubts and fears. Your aspiration in life should be to be the finest version of yourself.

Shifting Your Mindset

Our mind is so powerful and an important part of our body. The decision-making process begins in the mind. Do you want to work out? The mind might say, "Come on, let's just sleep for a little bit longer. My body still aches from yesterday". Or the mind might say, "Remember our fitness goals? Get up! We need to work out".

A positive mindset is important in achieving whatever goal you set for yourself. Whatever our goals are, we tend to doubt ourselves. I doubted myself a lot at the onset of my journey. This made it difficult for me to see the results that had developed from working out. I thought nothing was happening and that I was still the same as I had been. But I was wrong.

A negative mindset makes you doubt every step you take in your journey. You doubt that the vegetables are making any difference. You doubt that your arms are getting toned. This mindset also makes you compare yourself to others. You see changes in others and begin to doubt that you are doing the right thing. Eventually, a negative mindset will make you give up on your fitness goals and journey because it feels like a waste of time.

How do you develop a positive mindset?

- **Focusing on the positive things:** What are the rewards that could come from working out? To be physically fit to carry out work duties? Lower possibilities of being diagnosed with diabetes? Focus on these positive outcomes and your mindset will shift.

- **Spend time with positive people:** Have an intimate circle of people who support you. They are bound to lift you up whenever your mind strays toward negativity.

- **Practice positive self-talk:** Talk to yourself before you start working out and after your routine. Whenever you feel the negativity creep in, talk some positivity. You can record a voice note that you play when you feel low.

- **Identify areas of negativity:** What moments do you feel negativity creep in? Is it when you compare yourself with others? Or when the pain kicks in? By identifying these moments, you will understand that your mind is only trying to discourage you from being a better version of yourself.

- **Meditate:** You can meditate even in the midst of chaos. Close your eyes, take a deep breath, and let your body be free. Let the stress and pain fade out, and welcome in positivity as you let negativity out of your body and soul. Regular meditation before and in between workout sessions, as well as at the start and end of your day, will help shift your mindset to positivity.

Develop a positive mindset and even on days you don't feel up to it, you will be able to hit your target and even more.

In the next chapter, I will talk more about how you can practice self-care and how positivity serves as a major ingredient.

CHAPTER SUMMARY

- Your success will primarily rely upon effort
- Prioritizing helps you to concentrate your effort
- There should be a strategy for everything you do
- A positive mindset is important in achieving whatever goal you set for yourself

ACTION PLANS

1. As of now, I will begin to check my workflow to complete my assignments in total perfection.

2. As of now, I will _____

_____

_____

_____

_____

_____

_____

_____

_____

_____

_____

_____

_____

Give 110% to Everything You Do

"Every one of us needs to show how much we care for each other and, in the process, care for ourselves."

— PRINCESS DIANA

CHAPTER 4

Practice Self-Care

Aconsequence of becoming older is having more responsibility. You'll be asked to run errands for your spouse, look after a loved one, work extra hours to make ends meet, and pray that you make it to everyone's invitation for an occasional celebration. Due to the natural aging process, you might notice that you don't move as fast, you need more time to warm up before engaging in activities, and your knees make a clicking sound when walking down the stairs. You are not alone. I'm here to assure you. As you begin to grow into adulthood, make sure that you make time for yourself. Your boss, relative, and friends can be very demanding at times, and to be honest, you will not be able to please everyone. One thing that you can take control of is your well-being. Pouring from an empty cup is really challenging. As you prepare to work for an 8-hour shift, make sure that you are working as hard on yourself as you do at work. Becoming burnt out from work and toxic relationships will not only take a toll on you mentally but physically and spiritually. As I've previously stated, today's culture puts heavy emphasis on "securing the bag," but as you aspire for financial stability, make sure that you occasionally check in with your emotions and that you practice some form of self-care, whether it is listening to music, hanging out with friends, watching a movie, etc. As you maneuver through life, work, relationships, and so on, you will have to become your biggest advocate and take care of yourself.

Below are some self-care habits that I enjoy doing in my spare time:

Going for a Run: Every day, I try to exercise for at least 30 minutes. Sometimes I may need the extra push to get started, but once I've committed myself to my routine, it's one of the most rewarding things I can do for myself. Given my background in exercise science, I think that it is important that I practice what I preach. All I need is my Asics running shoes, and I'm willing to run at the local park or gym any day.

Spending Time in Nature: I love to go for a walk in the park or on a hiking trip with my friends. Being in nature can be soothing, and if you live in the inner city, you know that the combinations of cars, construction work and crowds can get very noisy. Being surrounded by water and trees and walking along the rocky trails can be fun and adventurous.

Attending Music Concerts: Being the rap nerd that I am, I find myself attending at least 2 concerts/festivals a year. Being able to sing along with your friends in a crowd of people who enjoy the same taste in music as you and having your favorite artist present is a wonderful experience. If Jeezy is to make an appearance in my nearby hometown, you better believe I'll make an effort to be there!

Making Music: It's no secret that music is one of my favorite things to make in my free time. Since I was young, making music has been therapeutic for me, and I enjoy the process of making something from scratch and seeing how people will react to you. In the past couple of years, I've released several music projects under my artist name, "Mo 804."

Reading Books: Whether it's self-help, spirituality, finances, autobiographies, history, or health books, I read them all. We have 24 hours in a day, and if someone can teach me or give me insight on a topic that I want to know, I am always eager to learn new information. I'd recommend reading at least 10 minutes. The answer you are looking for could be placed in a book.

Going to the movies: Even with the emergence of streaming services, going to the movies is something that I find relaxing. To me, the dimmed lights, buttery popcorn, and comfortable seats are like the equivalent of a spa. Watching a new movie on the big screen makes me feel that I am a part of the film. My interests in movies include Sci-fi, thriller, history, and comedy.

Eating my favorite foods: In the fall of 2016, I became a vegetarian. My transition from consuming meats to following a plant-based diet has forced me to make a conscious and concerted effort to consume foods that are nutrient-dense and that are good for my well-being. Curry Tofu with steamed vegetables, Drunken Noodles, Peanuts, Pears, and Chocolate-chip cookies are a few of my favorite things to eat.

Paying myself first: Every month, you will have to pay for rent/mortgage, utilities, car insurance, and other monthly bills, but when you first receive your paycheck, I recommend that you pay yourself first. This can be as little as 10% of your paycheck. You've worked hard for your money, and you deserve to enjoy the fruits of your labor. Pay your overhead, but don't forget to spoil yourself as well.

Getting my rest: I don't think there's one human on earth who doesn't enjoy snuggling up in their comfy bed. After a long day at work, I like to recharge with 30 minutes naps, and when possible, I enjoy a good night's sleep. Sometimes I say to myself, "you need 8 to be great," meaning that 8 hours of sleep is ideal for optimal health. It is true that when you do not get enough sleep, it's hard for the body to function.

In the previous chapter, I mentioned having a strategy as pertains to achieving goals, but something that is oftentimes overlooked is self-care. When you don't implement self-care, you run the risk of experiencing burnout. Do you find yourself in a work environment where the work demands are high, access to resources is low, and you find it difficult to maintain a work-life balance? Chances are you are experiencing burnout. To be honest, hustle culture is convincing at times and conveys messages that if you work hard, you too can become a millionaire. The drawback is that although many would like to reap the rewards of their hard work, being put under high amounts of pressure with limitations on time can lead to stress and the development of systemic disorders such as high blood pressure, high cholesterol, and diabetes. As cliché as it sounds, your health is literally your wealth. If you don't have the strength and energy to do your responsibilities, how likely are you to secure your financial future? My recommendation would be to create a "wellness check-in" where you can rate how you are feeling today and implement things that are non-work-related in your daily routine. If dancing is a part of your identity, try participating in a dance class. If you love making poetry, dedicate some time in your workweek towards writing. If you enjoy live music, attend the concert. Your identity is much bigger than the title of your job. You shouldn't wait until the weekend to live your life. Your health and mental well-being are your greatest assets and should be your top priority. If it requires the aid of a counselor, therapist, doctor, etc., then it is worth the investment. It is okay to be selfish when it comes to taking care of yourself.

As was already established, self-care is what we refer to as love. Your self-love will motivate you to pursue your goals without slacking off!

Since practically everything that has ever occurred in this world has been a result of love, love is the original success principle. There cannot possibly be a single life on this planet without love. Humans are created out of love, and they go on to create a wide variety of other things.

Successful people nearly always advise their followers who strive to become successful as well to "do what you love and enjoy what you do."

Although the expression has somehow lost some of its original meaning, it still has some valuable applications.

Why Positive Self Care Habits Are More Beneficial Than Negative Self Care Habits

Positive self-care has been clinically proven to reduce or eliminate anxiety and depression, and stress, improve concentration, minimize frustration and anger, increase happiness, improve energy, and more. Self-care has been clinically proven to reduce the risk of heart disease, stroke, and cancer. Spiritually, it may help us stay in touch with our higher power and realize our purpose in life – negative self-care habits will open way for more worries and problems.

Why We Should Avoid Bad Habits

Bad habits disrupt your life and prevent you from attaining your goals. They harm your health – both mentally and physically. And they waste your time and efforts.

Negative Self-Care Habits:

- Smoke/use tobacco
- Drink a lot of coffee or caffeinated drinks (more than 2-3 cups per day)

- Drink alcohol (more than recommended levels of 1-2 per day)
- Overuse over-the-counter medications
- Overeat or undereat
- Have angry outbursts
- Withdraw from people
- Ignore or deny stress symptoms
- Engage in self-destructive relationships

Positive Self-Care Habits:

- Live healthily (exercise five days a week for a minimum of 30 minutes)
- Practice good hygiene
- See friends regularly
- Try to do something you enjoy every day
- Find ways to relax (prayer/meditation)
- Eat a balanced diet
- See your doctor
- Express gratitude
- Hug your kid, spouse or pet

Why You Should Implement Positive Self-Talk Over Negative Self-Talk

According to research, positive self-talk can enhance well-being, stress management, and self-esteem; reduce any signs of personality problems, such as depression and anxiety; and aid in the treatment of eating disorders. Negative self-talk in any form must be avoided.

We have these numerous thoughts about ourselves, others, and the world at large and this can significantly impact what we say about others, our situations, and ourselves. Our thoughts influence what we say, and what we say defines how we do it piece by piece, step by step. These belief systems we build for ourselves are the result of a variety of experiences that we have had throughout our lives. One does not become a negative self-talker overnight; such a mindset takes years to develop, but the truth is not very encouraging. So many of us misinterpret life's circumstances, failures, and actions of others, and we tend to bring them on ourselves.

But, as we all know, negative self-talk is one of the worst mental traps that can lower and harm our self-esteem and others, even if it happens inadvertently. When you boldly declare something negative about yourself, it creeps into your framework of beliefs and eventually manifests in your life.

Attitude is changing things! You may recall Winston Churchill's famous quote: "Attitude is a tiny thing that makes a big difference." For instance, if you're nursing that negative thought about yourself as though you're not good enough, trust me, you won't be. It is so simple, yet many fall victim to negative thoughts. Examine what could be the core of your negative thoughts and try to figure out all the changes you need to make.

People are becoming increasingly conscious that positive self-talk is a strong technique for enhancing self-confidence and reducing negative feelings. People who have mastered positive self-talk are regarded as being more confident, motivated, and productive.

Practice Self-Care

When you are doing what you love, you will be thrilled and want to work harder in order to keep that happiness. When you are not doing what you love, you will easily become bored or give up, even if the task you are working on occasionally proves to be challenging.

Your motivation and drive to seek more, achieve more, and deliver more will increase.

There is a way if you just have the desire. Therefore, no matter what it takes to complete the task at hand, if you don't give up on what you do because you love doing it, you will succeed.

Self-care and loving oneself are the same. Knowing this, you want to be careful about the activities you choose to engage in, especially if you struggle with self-love.

Focusing on negative thoughts may lead to lower motivation as well as greater emotions of helplessness. This type of critical inner conversation has also been related to depression, so it's definitely something to fix. Those who find themselves constantly indulging in negative self-talk are likely to be more anxious.

The examples of positive and negative self-talk are shown in the chart below:

Positive Self Talk	Negative Self Talk
☐ It sounds challenging	☐ That is too difficult
☐ I will give it my best shot	☐ I cannot do it
☐ If i mess up, I will learn from it	☐ I always mess things up

Practicing self-care is important and how you manage your time is critical. Being time conscious will allow you to perform more tasks perfectly and attain your goals, which I will discuss in the following chapter. Let's move on to the next crucial topic.

CHAPTER SUMMARY

- Make time for yourself
- Create a wellness check-in
- Develop positive self-care habits
- It is okay to be selfish when it comes to taking care of yourself

ACTION PLANS

1. As of now, I will give priority to myself and whatever I want to lay my hands on.

2. As of now, I will _____

_____

_____

_____

_____

_____

_____

_____

_____

_____

_____

_____

_____

_____

IN DUE TIME

"The pessimist complains about the wind; the optimist expects it to change; the realist adjusts the sails."

– WILLIAM ARTHUR WARD

CHAPTER 5

Be Optimistic, But Be Realistic

Seeing the silver lining in a situation or expecting the best is only the beginning of optimism. It also serves as an explanation for what has previously occurred. Optimists consider what they did to influence the outcome when something positive occurs. They consider their gifts to be enduring, dependable pieces of who they are.

To be optimistic is to have a positive mindset. When you are faced with challenges, your mindset and approach can be pivotal to your success. "Is the glass half empty or half full" is a metaphorical expression of how the human mind perceives a situation. The "glass" represents life and its obstacles. Are you able to see the good in your current situation, or are you primarily focused on the negative? Your state of mind and the state of your condition are both factors. To be optimistic is not to say that you should not be realistic. Let's say that you are a professional athlete who is preparing for a big game. You've studied film and practiced numerous hours on your skills. On

Be Optimistic, But Be Realistic

game day, you should feel confident that you are capable of winning today's game. Allowing fear to seep into the mind will only render negative thoughts and self-doubt. Proverbs 23:7 states that "As a man thinketh, so is he." Ultimately, you have to believe you are a champion before becoming one. The honorable Marcus Garvey once stated that "if you have no confidence in self, you are twice defeated in the race of life." There are some exceptional cases where fear is needed, such as avoiding being attacked by a poisonous snake or the fear of falling from an unstable surface, but as it pertains to accomplishments, being fearful can lead to self-defeat.

As you aspire to achieve greatness, you will need to prioritize the things that matter most. There will be many distractions, but it is ultimately up to you if things are to get done. Some people have a tendency to rely heavily on positive affirmations, which can play a positive aspect on your mental well-being, but if it is not coupled with steps towards achieving your goals, you are absolutely going nowhere. In the bible, it mentions that faith without actions is dead – this statement is true. Let's say that you are an artist who wishes to make a million dollars from your art. You can use positive self-talk and proclaim that you are the best at what you do, but if you do not invest and perfect your craft, how will this happen? It is okay to be optimistic about your future, but you also have to be realistic about your circumstances. Once you are aware of who you are and your place in society, making and achieving goals become attainable. Most importantly, you should focus on making *SMART* goals that are Specific, Measurable,

Achievable, Relevant, and Time-Bound. For the artist who wants to make a million dollars, this may look like this:

- I want to increase my record sales by 10% by December 31st.
- I want to expand my audience number by 5% in 15 days by adopting social media advertising.
- I want to scale up my business by 25% in 3 months to establish a branch in downtown Richmond, Virginia.

As you can see with the aforementioned goals, the objective of accumulating a million dollars can be achieved with realistic, SMART goals.

Wallace "Wally" Amos Jr, the founder of the Famous Amos chocolate-chip cookies, opened his Famous Amos Cookie Store on Sunset Boulevard in Los Angeles in 1975. Inspired by his Aunt Della's chocolate-chip cookie recipe, he was able to accumulate massive amounts of success for nearly a decade, selling his version of the cookie. His optimism, unwavering faith, and commitment to making one of the world's most famous cookies in the 1970s led him to sell $300,000 worth of cookies in its first year, and by 1982, he was able to make $12 million in revenue. Prior to selling cookies, Wallace worked in show business as a talent agent, working with artists like Helen Reddy and Marvin Gaye, who would eventually become investors in the Famous Amos brand. The infamous bite-sized cookies were recognized by magazines, newspapers, and outlets as one of the best cookies in America. Famous Amos began to grow in popularity, and with the arrival of new competitors, Wallace struggled with the management of the Famous Amos Company. In 1984, Wallace began to sell shares of the Famous Amos Company to investors and would ultimately lose equity and control, which resulted in him selling the entire company for $3 million to Shansby Group in 1988. The shortcomings of Wallace's business can be attributed to his inability to keep up with the brand's rapid growth. In a recent interview, Wallace admitted that he did not have a business model in mind. Without a business model, Wallace was unequipped to deal with threats, which a SWOT analysis could have prevented. Indeed, Wallace's early success in building his cookie empire was fueled by optimism, but without specific, measurable, achievable, relevant, time-bound (SMART) goals, the future of the company would eventually crumble. Today the Famous Amos Brand is worth billions of dollars, and despite losing his company, Wallace Amos Jr. broke barriers with the launch of his premium chocolate chip cookie.

Setting Your Goals

Before becoming passionate about something, you must ascertain your objectives and the activities you find the most enjoyable. With this knowledge, you can create a professional path for yourself that will enable you to do what you love while also achieving your objectives.

However, regardless of how successful you have already been, how well educated you are, or what kind of personality you have, setting precise goals and working relentlessly toward reaching those goals are among the main recipes for success. Ensure your goals are your own and not ones placed on you as you define your personal, professional, and financial objectives.

You could get motivation or pressure to attain particular goals from your parents, spouse, friends, or other family members. However, it is crucial that the objectives you decide to pursue are ones you genuinely want to achieve for yourself. The pressure other people will put on you, such as a parent who wants you to follow in their footsteps, can occasionally be great and even overpowering. However, it would be best if you took responsibility for your actions and decisions to be happy and prosperous in the long run. Therefore, utilizing the suggestions, encouragement, and motivation of others is undoubtedly permissible and recommended.

You will find a way to accomplish the things that are essential to you. For things that you want to avoid, you will find an excuse. Excuses are self-defeating, and unless you have good reasoning for not doing something, then it is best to avoid excuses and hold yourself accountable for your actions. You need to be realistic about the kind of goals you set – we have Long-term and short-term goals, which are two different categories. The criterion of time applies to both types of goals. While short-term goals can be achieved in a month, week, or day, long-term goals may span a decade, twenty years, or even a lifetime. People who are good at making goals frequently align their short-term and long-term objectives to help them stay focused on one course of action.

Be Optimistic, But Be Realistic

Setting objectives is fundamental, and there are many different strategies for doing so that all focus on the SMART qualities. Remember, Specific, Measurable, Achievable, Relevant, and Time-bound are all acronyms for SMART goals.

Pen down the specific goals you have for yourself in the following three areas: personal, professional, and financial, based on where you are in your life right now. Consider a short-term objective as something you wish to accomplish in the next 12 months to keep things straightforward. Something that will take more than a year to accomplish is a long-term objective.

Make sure your goals are reasonable when you write them down. For instance, if your goal is to design and build fine furniture, but you are currently making a comfortable living as an Accountant, you must be very realistic about the financial sacrifice you will be making, at least in the short term, as well as the challenges you may face by choosing this less common career path. Being realistic will enable you to concentrate your efforts and provide your goals with a strong base upon which to be built.

You might need to rethink certain overly ambitious goals if you do a realistic assessment of the risks, effort required, and possibilities of achievement. Make sure your objectives can be achieved with the risk and effort that you are comfortable taking.

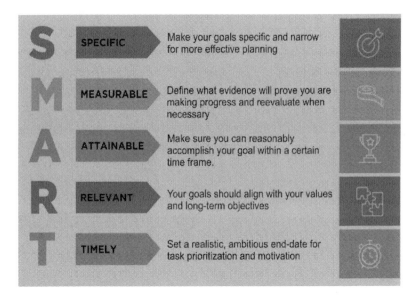

Encourage Yourself or Stay Motivated

When it comes to keeping fit, I would be lying if I said the journey is easy. Trust me, I don't mean to scare you, but it is difficult, especially when you are just starting. Eventually, it gets easier, but never easy.

There will be moments you just want to lay in bed and do nothing. Times you think staying a week from the gym is the best thing to do. Sometimes you wonder if the fitness journey is even worth it. This will happen at several stages, from being a beginner to being an advanced fitness enthusiast.

You are your greatest fan. You have to encourage yourself and stay motivated. Otherwise, you will give up and have all you have worked for be in vain. I have seen people easily give up, when all they need is some motivation to keep them on the journey.

Be Optimistic, But Be Realistic

How do you stay motivated?

- **Appreciate your wins:** No matter how little it may seem to lift a small dumbbell, appreciate it. Where you are now, you weren't there a couple of weeks ago. Take pride in your wins and create new targets.
- **Believe that you can:** Nothing is impossible. I mean, you may not compete for the next weightlifting challenge, but you know if you're dedicated and put your mind to it, you actually can? Your targets may seem impossible, but think back on those seemingly difficult things that you now do with ease. You can do it once you put your mind to it.
- **Break down your tasks into smaller parts:** As a whole, you may feel discouraged, but by doing 5 reps at a time, with a 2 minutes break, you will be easily motivated to finish the sets.
- **Reward yourself:** Reward yourself for accomplishing wins. But these rewards should not be opposed to your goals, like skipping a workday or snacking on junk food. It could be a pedicure or manicure or buying a book. When you know there's a reward, you will be easily motivated to meet your targets.
- **Be proud of yourself:** One thing I did to encourage myself when I felt discouraged was to look within myself and be proud of my wins. I would stare at myself in the mirror and flex my muscles. I would look at before and after pictures and see how far I had come; I was proud of myself.

- **Have a role model or mentor:** Look up to someone with a similar journey. This could be a family member, colleague at work, friend, or public figure. You do not have to have an intimate relationship with this person. However, strive for one. You will be encouraged by seeing the steps this person took to a healthier life.

Look at the bigger picture. Do you like what you see? Yes, you do. Keep on moving, and you will be a better version of who you are right now.

From here, we will look at the importance of collaboration and why 2 brains are better than 1.

CHAPTER SUMMARY

- To be optimistic is to have a positive mindset
- Create SMART goals
- It is okay to be optimistic about your future, but you also must be realistic about your circumstances.

ACTION PLANS

1. As of now, I will focus on my strengths and not my weaknesses.

2. As of now, I will _____

_____

_____

_____

_____

_____

_____

_____

_____

_____

_____

_____

IN DUE TIME

"Two heads are better than one, not because either is infallible, but because they are unlikely to go wrong in the same direction."

– C. S. LEWIS

CHAPTER 6

Collaborate: 2 Brains Are Better Than 1

In my younger years, football was a part of my identity. In the game of football, much of your success has to do with how you play collectively as opposed to individual performance. Although quarterbacks, wide receivers, and running back may be recognized in media for the fashion in which they score sports, as a unit, each of the 11 players must be on the same page in order to execute the play. The offensive linemen whose job is to protect the quarterback can ruin a play if any one of the players does not complete their assignment. Being introduced to teamwork from playing organized football made me realize that such is the game of life. In many aspects, you will have to rely on your family, community, and social groups in order to achieve the greater good of what is needed in society. Truly, teamwork makes the dream work. What we have today is the manifestation of things that people agreed upon. Yes, being intelligent may help you to excel individually, but efforts in collaborative problem-solving can leave an imprint on society. There is an African proverb that goes, "Go alone if you want to go fast. If you want to go far, go together," and this I believe rings true in school, business, home, etc.

When I was in undergrad and grad school, I would often study with my classmates. As obvious as this may sound, many intelligent people are sometimes reluctant to form study groups. Some scholars (not all) are capable of achieving independent success. Many of these self-reliant habits were formed in high school or even middle school. In college, the work demand is higher and requires you to grasp concepts at an expedited pace.

For this reason, 2 brains are better than 1. There are some subject matters that you will find intriguing, and others will be boring. Those that you find to be mundane, your classmate may find exciting. As humans, we all have different learning styles, which makes us unique. I personally was more of a visual learner, so I would often find diagrams, graphs, drawings, etc. To be more helpful than listening (auditory) or acting out things (kinesthetic). The beauty in this is that your team or study group will have their strengths, and overall, this increases the collective intelligence of the group.

What you were able to learn in 5 minutes may have taken me 5 hours, and with this type of collaborative effort, we can share what we know and agree on the correct answer or decision. Collaboration works just as well in work meetings, sports organizations, and religious circles.

IN DUE TIME

In life, you will experience victory and losses. For some people, winning requires a group effort, and in some cases, it requires a determination by the individual.

Venus and Serena Williams, two professional American women tennis players, have won multiple grand slams and are regarded as two of the best tennis players in the history of the sport. The two sisters both grew up in Compton, California, where they learned to play the game of tennis from their father, Richard Williams. Inspired by the tennis match victory won by Virginia Ruzici in 1977, Richard Williams wrote a 78-page manifesto detailing the plans for his daughter's success. Both Richard and his former wife, Oracene Price, would assist in coaching Venus and Serena Williams in the fundamentals of tennis while building their self-esteem. This collective effort in brain power is what leads to both Venus and Serena Williams winning numerous grand slams and Olympic matches. Surprisingly, neither Richard Williams nor Oracene Price were professional tennis players. Their admiration for the game and commitment to bettering the lives of their two daughters under challenging circumstances in Compton is what led them to create two of the greatest athletes in the world. Richard Williams has spoken on numerous occasions of how he would get into physical altercations with local gang members in order for his daughters to have access to public tennis courts. Eventually, the gang members of the community would accept the Williams Sisters and had a newfound respect for Richard Williams. The Williams family had a plan in mind, and as the saying goes, "a plan without a plan is just a wish."

Collaborate: 2 Brains Are Better Than 1

You should share your thoughts with those who share your desire for achievement when setting goals. This point stands out among the concepts that direct our quest to accomplish our objectives for a number of reasons. Your idea alone is not enough, you can share it with other people in your circle, and they will add to it to make it work out faster.

As we all know, teamwork is what makes a dream come true, but the level of understanding inside the team will determine how successful it is. For you to continue making progress and consistently attaining success, having someone else to make sure you stay on track is essential. Don't overlook the power of others, the way you see things is different from how others will see them. A figure 9 may look like a figure 6 to another person based on how you perceive it. Below are some examples of the benefits of collaborative teamwork and the limitations of individual work:

Collaborative teamwork	Individual work
▮	▮
☐ Encourages problem-solving	☐ Difficult to solve problem alone
☐ Learn from each other	☐ No access to other people's opinion
☐ Productivity rates go up	☐ Limited production output

You should share your thoughts with those who share your desire for achievement when setting goals. This point stands out among the concepts that direct our quest to accomplish our objectives for a number of reasons: your idea alone is not enough, you can share it with other people in your circle, and they will add to it to make it work out faster.

As we all know, teamwork is what makes a dream come true, but the level of understanding inside the team will determine how successful it is. To continue to make progress and consistently attain success, having someone else to collaborate with is essential to staying on track.

CHAPTER SUMMARY

- Teamwork makes the dream work
- You will have to rely on your family, community, and social groups to achieve success
- Your team or study group will have their strengths

ACTION PLANS

1. As of now, I will find a like mind to reason with for the betterment and a smooth journey to reach my destination goal.

2. As of now, I will _____

_____

_____

_____

_____

_____

_____

_____

_____

_____

_____

_____

IN DUE TIME

"The key to immortality is first living a life worth remembering."

— BRUCE LEE

CHAPTER 7

Know Your Worth

Whether you believe it or not, you are worthy. The fact that you are here in this present moment is a clear indication that you are special. Out of 250 million sperm cells, only one sperm cell can be the successor that fertilizes the egg. From conception to birth, you were being created for this very moment. Upon birth, every one of us is classified by social constructs and identified by our chromosome makeup. Within this lifetime, there will be opportunities to win, fail and, most importantly, learn. Although winning is glorified, there is always a lesson within failure. Without failure, we wouldn't appreciate winning. To fail doesn't mean that you are a failure; it is simply an opportunity to correct your mistakes. Despite the shortcoming, pitfalls, and mishaps, life is something that is worth the experience. You are valuable, and if/when you can recognize this, you will have to move accordingly. Even in the midst of economic poverty and financial hardships, you still have a culture that is worth millions. For example, Black Americans created Hip-Hop, which was created out of the slums of the Bronx and is now worth billions today. Soul Food, another Black American invention, was literally conceptualized out of deprivation. Many of the enslaved Africans in the Americas were given "scraps" or "waste" and were able to make famous dishes such as chitterlings, fried chicken, macaroni, cheese, etc. In spite of it all, we, as a culture, are able to make lemonade out of lemons.

Viola Davis, an African American actress and producer, has spoken on several occasions of her humble beginnings. Raised in Central Falls, Rhode Island, the actor often experienced poverty, dysfunction, and instability. In recent interviews, Davis spoke about living in harsh conditions, where she would search for food in trash bins and sleep in dilapidated, rat-infested apartments in Central Falls, which was considered one of the poorest cities in the 1970s. Growing up impoverished, Davis often felt "invisible" and unseen by others. By the time she reached high school, she had grown an interest in acting, a career and opportunity that would help to escape the dark reality of the world that she lived in. She earned a scholarship to study theatre at Rhode Island College and to attend the Juilliard school in New York City. In 1996 she made her first screen debut as a nurse in the film *Substance of Fire*. Davis was not content with playing supporting roles, and she knew she was worthy of more. By 2001 she had advanced to bigger roles and received many accolades, which included the Tony award, an award given to actors for their excellence in live Broadway performances. In 2008, she had a breakthrough after starring in a film called *Doubt*, receiving nominations for her performance. The little girl that was born on her grandma's farm in Saint Matthews, South Carolina, who once felt invisible, was becoming an icon in the public eye. In 2015, Davis became the first Black Woman to win an Emmy for best actress in a drama series. Davis admitted in publications that knowing her worth has been a struggle, but the day she recognized she was worthy, her entire life changed. Today, Davis is 1 of 24 actors who have won the Triple Crown of acting (which includes the Tony, Oscar Emmy), setting her apart from the competition. In one of her acceptance speeches, Davis recalls a common saying that goes, "the two most important days in one's life are the day you were born and the day you discover why you were born." Viola Davis continues to walk in her life's purpose.

Knowing your worth allows you to dictate your life. You are the captain of your ship, and you have to determine which direction you will want to go. There will be times in life when you will have to make tough decisions, and it may require you to stand up for yourself. Though this may sound intimidating, when you voice your emotions, this act can be empowering for not only you but for generations to follow. The freedom we enjoy today is contingent upon the sacrifices of humans who were willing to challenge the status quo. Zora Neal Hurston once stated that "if you are silent about your pain, they'll kill you and say you enjoyed it." collectively, the strength is in numbers. What good is individual success if we are unable to push our culture forward? This is not to say everyone has to be an activist or become a martyr for a cause, but everyone is worthy and has something to offer to humanity. In life, we are given choices. The choices that you make reflect actions which in turn become habits that ultimately define your character. As Dr. Martin Luther King Jr once stated, "The ultimate measure of a man is not where he stands in moments of comfort and convenience, but where he stands at times of challenge and controversy." Know your worth and produce justice.

You should also continue to analyze frequently. Take time to evaluate or reflect on the following three items periodically while you work toward your ultimate goal:

1. What are you doing?
2. What methods are effective?
3. What areas do you require assistance in?

After taking care of these issues, make the required adjustments to speed up your progress. People could become fixated on doing what they believe they ought to do in order to achieve their objective. They frequently don't stop to think about what they're doing, which can greatly slow down their progress or completely throw them off track, preventing them from ever achieving their goal.

Regularly evaluate what you're doing to help you attain your goal more quickly and succeed at a higher level in less time. Below I will list some positive affirmations that are important and can help you to mentally balance or recognize your worth and value.

Positive Affirmations

- I am love. I am purpose. I was made with divine intention
- I am worthy of what I desire
- I can. I will. End of story
- I am adventurous. I overcome fears by following my dreams
- I feed my spirit. I train my body. I focus my mind. It's my time
- I am in charge of my life
- I am the hero of my own life

CHAPTER SUMMARY

- You are worthy
- To fail doesn't mean you are a failure
- Knowing your worth allows you to dictate your life

ACTION PLANS

1. As of now, I will keep evaluating my progress to know what I have left to do.

2. As of now, I will _____

_____

_____

_____

_____

_____

_____

_____

_____

_____

_____

_____

_____

_____

IN DUE TIME

"Success isn't always about greatness. It's about consistency. Consistent hard work leads to success. Greatness will come."

– DWAYNE JOHNSON

CHAPTER 8

Be Consistent

Everything that has value in life is a product of consistency. As mentioned previously, you should give 110% in everything that you but you must continue to do this on a consistent basis. The world marvels at how Lebron James is able to play at such a high level this late into his career, but what most do not realize is that Lebron is consistently hitting the weight room, adhering to his diet regimen, and figuring out ways to enhance his performance. Anybody in the NBA has the capability of scoring 30 points in a night. But what separates a good player from a superstar is their ability to do this on a consistent basis. When I decided to participate in my first 10K race, I didn't know what to expect. However, I was determined to make it to the finish line. Months prior to the race, I would form a schedule and make it a habit to run 2-3 times per week. Day in and day out, I would work on perfecting this new craft that I wasn't quite accustomed to. Growing up, I primarily played football, which included physical contact with other players and required a different set of skills to be successful.

Be Consistent

Nevertheless, I began my journey into running in an effort to live a healthier lifestyle and formed a schedule that I would follow religiously. There were days that I was I was sore, achy, and sleepy, but I did not quit. As a result, I lost weight in the process, which gave me a boost in motivation to stay consistent. I knew that I had a goal to run a 10K (approximately 6.2 miles) and that it would require my effort to show up for training, even on the days I didn't feel like it. It will be days that you will not feel inspired, but you must stay focused in remain the course.

To be consistent means that you hold yourself accountable. Accountability means that you take ownership of your actions. For some, this can be quite difficult. When things don't go our way in life, it's easy to blame others for why you are not where you are in life. As my mother would often say, "When you point the finger, you have three pointing back at you." Granted, there are some circumstances that are out of our control. For instance, you cannot control the weather.

There will be rainy days, and there will be sunny days, but life goes on. You can't control traffic, but you can make a concerted effort to wake up earlier. You can't control the past, but you can examine your current actions and properly plan for the future. As the late great Maya Angelou once stated, "If you don't like something, change it. If you can't change it, change your attitude". This simple yet powerful statement holds true to any obstacles that you may be facing at this moment. It's okay to make mistakes. Sooner or later in life, you will fail at something. The best thing that you can do is to learn from those mistakes, re-adjust your focus and stay consistent with your plan.

IN DUE TIME

This consistency principle largely revolves around regularity. With the exception of winning the lottery or inheriting money, success does not happen overnight. It demands everyone concerned to put up 110% effort. Unfortunately, not many people are willing to make such sacrifices; thus, some have difficulty achieving success.

Success is more a process than a thing, more like accumulation than attainment. You must put in consistent effort in addition to doing the right thing if you want to succeed in your life's goals. Many people enjoy setting objectives but are unable to carry them out since a good daily routine is not created. A daily routine is just a list of things you can do to achieve your goal on a daily basis. For instance, if you want to build enormous muscles, your routine can include going to the gym every day or once a week, following a diet, eating well, and other things. Let's examine Joe's gym goal. He has continuously attended the gym for the past six months based on his six-day per week plan, with no absences. He has successfully "trained" day by day, increasing his muscle mass from small to large.

Actually, consistency is a natural law. A tree requires proper care to grow, including watering, fertilizer application, and other practices. It is a daily action rather than an occasional event. You have to perform the same task repeatedly, which can be exhausting for some people.

Many people who are trying to succeed quit up along the way because they can't tolerate having to keep doing the same things

Be Consistent

over and over again without seeing any real progress. In actuality, success is attained in this way.

There are very few pushes that guarantee a result, but if you press frequently enough, many or all of your pushes will produce rewards for you.

Therefore, instead of considering giving up over some mundane, uninteresting duties, encourage yourself by picturing how joyful your life will be once you achieve your goal. All in all, stay with your plan; don't give up until you've reached your objective since losers always give up, but victors never do.

Because persistence and consistency go hand in hand, the latter must also be used. Despite the difficult challenges you may face, you must continue to persevere, especially if it is something that you love to do.

Perseverance is a success principle that cannot be overlooked, which encourages us to keep going even when things are difficult and reminds us to have a more resilient attitude than the difficulty of the work we are doing. The title of Dr. Robert H. Schuller's best-selling book, "Tough Times Never Last, But Tough People Do," best captures this.

Love is another success principle that could be strengthened by persistence and is somewhat related to it. High levels of devotion and perseverance accompany great affection.

For example, my friend Dan has found his passion in creating digital content. He has been so dedicated to working for two hours each day, six days a week, for the past six months in order to create amazing tutorial content to solve the specific problem in his chosen niche. In fact, he is so determined to create the best digital content that he has canceled numerous personal events. Instead of parties and public gatherings, he has become obsessed with his passion for web design. Because of his love for content creation, he has made tremendous progress in developing a website in less than six months. Thus, I think he has succeeded in his goal.

It takes a lot of effort to be persistent in anything you undertake. To develop persistence, you must possess it or engage in a variety of activities, such as:

1. First, love what you do.
2. Secondly, you need a goal that is specific, measurable, doable, practical, and time-bound. You might not have a compelling enough reason to stick with what you're doing when adversity arises if you don't have a SMART goal. You can combat the sense of giving up that keeps plaguing you by setting a SMART goal.
3. Extrinsic and intrinsic motivation are required. When you're feeling low, practice being kind to yourself by reminding yourself of the goal you must reach no matter what. Find something or someone to motivate you if you have trouble motivating yourself. It should be related to your aim, or someone should bring up your goal.

You need a good daily routine in order to make the journey successful.

Be Consistent

A good daily routine is a schedule of daily tasks that you follow in order to actualize your dreams or reach your goals. A goal is a goal, and it will never be achieved unless certain actions are regularly taken.

Success or failure depends on the frequent actions you take. Consequently, you should plan these activities in addition to your goals. Before they become overbearing, keep an eye on them.

Embrace Your Journey

The journey to a healthier life is a lifelong one. This is something you must realize. It is not something you get on, get off, then get back on. Do people do this? Yes, but they only create instability for themselves because just as the body gets settled down to a routine, they pull it off. Living a healthy life is a commitment that needs to be taken seriously.

This journey is not a dress that you take on. I wouldn't even call it a lifestyle. It is a part of you. Being fit is essential for your day-to-day activities, and as you do this, you will realize how it influences other areas of your life. In your workplace, you will be productive. Exercise boosts our moods, preventing depression. It makes us agile and fast-thinking.

Our journeys are all different. And this does not just apply to fitness. We are not the same. We may even start at the same time but will get different results. Every one of us is different, just as we have different DNA. It is so easy to compare our journey with others. You begin to wonder what you are doing wrong. Please, don't do this.

Remember that we have different body sizes. Our metabolisms are also different. What works for A might not work for B. This is why you should know your body well.

Your fitness journey to meet your targets may take time. For others, it may take a shorter time. Whatever the case may be, embrace your journey. Through the ups and downs, own it. Realize that it is an important phase you have to experience for greater goals.

Here are five tips to enjoy and embrace your journey:

- **Realize that this is a journey:** It is not a race. Just as it took you years to get to where you are fitness-wise, it would also take you some time to get rid of that body weight. Trust the process. Do not expect change to happen overnight.
- **Have a support system:** This could be people with similar fitness goals. Or friends and family who will rally around and support you to fulfill your fitness goals.
- **Keep track of your progress:** This way, you get to see the changes made over time in your journey. This will encourage and motivate you to keep on pushing and to enjoy the process.
- **Be realistic with your goals:** Having the perfect body is not realistic because different societies have different standards or concepts of what a "perfect" body should be. Instead, strive for a healthier body. Also, don't expect

results to happen overnight. What you give in is what you will get in results.

- **Focus on the journey:** Don't get too consumed with losing weight that all you want to do is stand on the scale and see a different number. You might end up getting disappointed. The goal is to be healthy. I once read a quote that said, "the man who loves walking, will walk further than the man who loves the destination." I find this to be a true statement.
- Being fit is a life-long commitment with beneficial results. It is a journey that I have been excited about. Make a move today.

CHAPTER SUMMARY

- Everything that has value in life is a product of consistency
- You will not always feel inspired, but you must stay focused and remain on course.
- To be consistent means that you hold yourself accountable

ACTION PLANS

1. As of now, I will keep doing what will yield me success, no matter the obstacle.

2. As of now, I will _____

_____

_____

_____

_____

_____

_____

_____

_____

_____

_____

_____

_____

_____

Be Consistent

"Good, better, best. Never let it rest. Until your good becomes better and better becomes best."

– ST JEROME

CHAPTER 9

Do Your Best

When you are focused on your goals, it is necessary that you do your best. Time and exposure are factors that determine your best. The more time and exposure you have to a particular area of study, the more likely you are to succeed. As my neurobiology professor would say, "It all takes repetition and saturation." When you are preparing for a test, you are given access to information you need to know in order to pass. Granted, some exams are harder than others, and it is up to you to prioritize what is most important. I've personally struggled with standardized exams and have failed on numerous occasions.

Do standardized exams reflect how intelligent you are? Of course not. Before I was accepted into Physical Therapy school in 2019, I was rejected twice; my poor standardized exam scores were partly to blame, but I did not let this deter me, and I continued to get better. By no means is this book to belittle the importance of standardized exams, as they are used as benchmarks in competency. However, what's important is that you do your best and understand that your best can vary when you have more time and exposure.

Aisha Cole, the owner and operator of Slutty Vegan, a plant-based burger restaurant chain in Atlanta, Georgia, has spoken openly about her past entrepreneurial mishaps. Prior to the launch of Slutty Vegan, the Baltimore native opened a Jamaican American eatery in Harlem, New York, in 2014, which was destroyed by a grease fire in 2016. Given her inexperience as a restaurant owner, she didn't have the proper form of insurance to cover such a catastrophe, which resulted in her being evicted from her apartment in New York, having her car repossessed, and losing an income of $35,000 a month. Having a background in television production, she decided to move to Los Angeles from New York to work as a casting director. After 2 years, she relocated to Atlanta and continued to work as a full-time employee with the same television company. In 2018, she decided to step back into the food industry, creating Slutty Vegan as a side hustle. During her part-time, she'd worked inside a commercial kitchen, perfecting her vegan burgers and sharing them with her friends. With the support of social media, her new business venture was starting to gain momentum, and customers were hungry for more. A few months later, she was fired from her full-time job due to the high demands of her new business, Slutty Vegan, and she decided to expand to a food truck service and finally to a brick-and-mortar in the southwest region of Atlanta in 2019. In less than six months, Cole became a millionaire. The moral of the story is that Aisha "Pinky" Cole could've quit during her first failure in 2016, but she didn't. To some people, her attempt in 2014 was a travesty and a complete waste of time. For her, this was an opportunity to learn from her mistakes and to become better. She continued to stay the course, and today she is one of the biggest influencers of vegan culture within the black community. Whether it is your first, second, or third attempt, keep going. Your best will always vary.

The best that you could do in 2016 is different from your best in 2022, and so on. Like many of us, we form new habits and ideas, and most importantly, we grow. With time and exposure, we are destined to evolve. Having the opportunity to wake up every day gives birth to new opportunities.

What you couldn't master in 30 days can be mastered in 90 days. What you can't accomplish in 90 days can be completed in 120 days. In life, mistakes are bound to happen. If you can learn from those mistakes, you will always win. Repeating the same mistakes and being unwilling to learn from them is a recipe for failure.

From this day forward, make sure that you do your best. At times, it can be frustrating when you do not get the results you wished for, but as the saying goes, "so far, you've survived 100% of your worst days, so this too shall pass." Anything worth having is worth fighting for, and in due time, you will get what your heart desires.

In order to be the best, you must be willing to learn from the best. There are likely people who came before you who have mastered an industry that you are working towards being a part of. Do not allow pride or ego to prevent you from learning from your predecessors.

Kobe Bryant, a 5-time NBA champion and Hall of Famer, would often study film and receive advice from Michael Jordan, a 6-time NBA champion and Hall of Famer. Both players were dominant figures in two separate eras.

The wisdom that Michael Jordan was able to give to a novice Kobe Bryant resulted in him being able to accumulate many accolades and become a household name in basketball. This is not to say that another individual should be solely credited for your hard work and success. However, the example mentioned above best demonstrates how iron can sharpen iron. Today, there are many players who idolize Kobe Bryant and look to him for inspiration. What you put out comes back to you. Just as Michael Jordan and Kobe Bryant were able to provide guidance for those who followed after them, so can you. Your best as a student, artist, musician, actor, entertainer, or even with responsibilities such as being a parent will vary with time.

The power and strength we have to comprehend life's matters are different. As a result, the outcomes of various endeavors may differ. Though success is never measured by brawn but by brain. Only the wise can dance to the tune of life. The way we see things is also different, and the kind of perspective we follow to act or react to what we see is also varied, which will make the outcome be of a different nature. Even if twins are born on the same day and are identical, many aspects of their lives will differ. Looking toward those who are already above you will give you a hint as to what has occurred. Learning from the legend is a blessing because there are lessons of glory in history.

Do not overlook the power of seeking the attention of superiors—the fact is that they know more than you. If you seek, they will tell, but if you think you know it all, their strategy will stick around them. If care is not taken, they will take the secret to their graveyard.

> **CHAPTER SUMMARY**
>
> - Factors that determine your best are time and exposure
> - Having the opportunity to wake up every day gives birth to new opportunities
> - Learning from your successors.

ACTION PLANS

1. As of now, I will strive always to do my best.

2. As of now, I will _____

_____

_____

_____

_____

_____

_____

_____

_____

_____

_____

_____

_____

_____

Do Your Best

PART 2

"Networking is an investment in your business. It takes time and when done correctly can yield great results for years to come."

- DIANE HELBIG

CHAPTER 10

Developing Your Network

It takes more than working hard, having the right knowledge, having a good education, and having the right talents to succeed. It also concerns your network and how you use your contacts. You will meet many individuals in your personal and professional life. Each person has a unique network of contacts, a body of information, and a set of abilities. You can learn how to use other people's resources by networking.

Based on the type of work you do, there is a good probability that success will involve other people—people in your network—in some way (directly or indirectly). Bosses, coworkers, subordinates, clients, friends, and anyone you see daily can all easily join your ever-expanding network.

Tapping Into Your Network

You probably ask individuals you know for recommendations when you decide to buy an expensive product, such as a new appliance, new automobile, or when you need to hire a lawyer, doctor, or contractor, for example. After all, you are more likely to believe a reference from a friend, relative, or coworker than one from a Yellow Pages advertisement. One simple method of networking to access the expertise of people you know to gain trustworthy information is to ask someone you know for a recommendation.

You can find new clients or customers, unlisted job positions, information, or opportunities through networking that you might not otherwise have access to.

You should continually be expanding your network, just as you should always be working toward reaching your long-term financial, professional, and personal goals. There are several fairly simple ways to accomplish this.

As you build up your network, you'll need to tap your social skills, interact with people, strike up conversations with strangers, and become a good listener. When you meet someone new, ask questions and make conversation in an effort to learn more about the person. Demonstrate a genuine interest in what the person has to say, and exchange business cards in the process of meeting new people. You never know if the person you just met might someday become a valuable new customer or client, be able to provide a referral or offer you some type of new opportunity.

There are several methods for expanding your network by meeting new individuals. Start by talking to your current friends, coworkers, business partners, and family members. Consider attending trade exhibitions and meetings sponsored by various professional organizations or associations to network with more individuals in your sector, for instance.

Volunteering, participating in church or temple activities, attending Chamber of Commerce events, getting engaged in local or regional politics, or attending social gatherings planned by friends are great ways to meet new people.

Offering suggestions or referrals and seeking them out is a necessary networking component. Keeping tabs on people is crucial as you grow your network. The most effective approach is gathering business cards and creating an extensive database of contact details. However, saving contact information using an electronic address book or contact management software program is a great option if you are comfortable with a computer or a PDA (like the Palm V). The benefits of keeping a well-organized contact database will outweigh the few minutes it takes to input a new person's name, address, phone number, and other details over time, but maintaining one will require some discipline and time on your part.

Having a strong network can be quite beneficial, for instance, when you require information or need to locate someone with expertise or understanding in a particular field. Similar to this, a personal introduction is one of the finest ways to get a job if you are seeking a certain industry or firm. There are scenarios where even if you do not directly know someone who can assist you, someone in your network probably knows someone who does. Effective networking includes getting and giving referrals as well as using the contacts of individuals you already know.

Developing Your Networking Skills

It is entirely up to you how hard you work to continuously develop and use your network. Expanding your network can be simple and even enjoyable if you are confident talking to strangers and striking up conversations. For instance, start a conversation with the passenger seated next to you on the plane if you are traveling alone for business. If you work out at a health club, talk to the individual next to you on the treadmill. However, you cannot predict when you will run into someone fascinating.

There are numerous books, videos, and audio courses that can help you hone your verbal communication abilities and feel more at ease engaging in conversations with strangers. This includes developing your self-confidence, your ability to ask the right questions, and your listening skills.

When you first someone for the first time, there is a good chance that person also finds starting an intellectual discussion awkward. What you talk about first is unimportant. You can talk about the weather, current affairs, a movie or TV show you have seen, a book you have read, the clothing a new acquaintance is sporting, your jobs, your family, or the performance of a sports team. The secret is to identify your shared interests with the other individual and then capitalize on them.

Communicating effectively is essential in developing networking skills. Be clear to the other person that you are approachable, outgoing, honest, and interested in what they have to say when you participate in conversations. You may utilize all of these to project the right image and improve your communication skills throughout a conversation, including what you say, how you say it, and your body language (including eye contact).

Keeping In Touch with Your Network

The process of developing your network never ends. While networking is crucial, you should also keep up with your current acquaintances personally and professionally. The most significant members of your network should get your full attention, but to maintain other connections, think about sending occasional personalized e-mails, notes, or other correspondence.

Sending Christmas, holiday, or New Year's cards throughout the holidays is one of the best ways to connect with people personally. For example, sending a card demonstrates your concern for their connection, even though it is not as personal as an in-person visit over lunch or dinner.

It is possible to have holiday cards printed professionally, but each card should have a unique, handwritten message and be signed. However, it is a good approach to put your business card in the envelope when sending cards to people you know in the business world.

You will ultimately need to set and accomplish your personal and professional goals on your own. But having a network in place can offer resources and assistance, which will simplify the process of succeeding. No matter what your career is, you will be better off the more people you know and the more people who respect, like, and consider you a friend.

Utilizing Your Network

You can use your network relationships not only to assist you in accessing untapped job markets but also to find new customers or clients, obtain information, connect with industry leaders, or locate people with certain abilities. Generally speaking, when using your network's resources, you should treat your connections with the utmost respect, especially if you are requesting a favor.

Never ask for too much or stress someone out to the point where they do not want to help you (or regret it afterward). Always express your gratitude for the person's support, both verbally and in a follow-up thank you note, and offer your help should it be required in the future. Assume that when you get in touch with someone in your network, they are preoccupied with their personal and professional obligations.

Do not continuously bother someone, for instance, by repeatedly sending emails or leaving voicemails. Instead, try leaving a single fax or email message as a follow-up to your voicemail message if you cannot get through to the individual immediately. Then, wait for them to get in touch with you.

As you start to use your network, you will probably discover that most people are happy to assist others if they are politely asked. Of course, there will always be a small percentage of people interested in the benefits themselves. Still, the majority of people enjoy being able to assist others by drawing on their expertise, contacts, or other resources, provided that doing so does not take up too much of their time or resources.

CHAPTER SUMMARY

- Networking is an essential ingredient to success
- One simple method of networking is to ask someone you know for a recommendation
- When using your network's resources, you should treat your connections with the utmost respect

ACTION PLANS

1. As of now, I will develop a network with like-minded people.

2. As of now, I will _____

_____

_____

_____

_____

_____

_____

_____

_____

_____

_____

_____

_____

_____

Developing Your Network

"Productivity is being able to do things that you were never able to do before."

– FRANZ KAFKA

CHAPTER 11

Embrace Productivity

You cannot expect to be more productive suddenly. However, you have likely spent years cultivating your good and bad job habits, consciously or subconsciously, and those are not going to change instantly.

Small adjustments may result in long-lasting changes, but they may take time and discipline. When you read a book like this, it feels really simple to believe it's simple. But that's not it, not from an expert perspective, but as a fellow employee in the fight against unproductivity.

How To Be More Productive

Make a reasonable to-do list: Don't get overwhelmed. To-do lists often fail due to the fact that we make them too complex. Some assignments are going to take a long time, and others are not going to take any time. This generates an imbalance in how we spread our time. Then what happens is that our to-do list becomes an instrument for procrastination. Yes, that's okay.

Because we do the simple things then, and then get really distracted about the difficult things.

You did that before, don't lie. So, you have to.

Set tiny task objectives: The scope may seem too large with each new project or assignment. Once you start to break it down and realize what can be done, you will realize how each component builds on the other.

For example, one of the most practical and simplest things you can do is break down your big marketing or deliverable project into smaller objectives. What are the necessary pieces and assets? Who do you first need to speak to? Break these parts before setting timelines, then estimate how long they're going to take you to complete. Understanding the scope of what is being asked, setting up the steps, and then estimating the time needed will help you gain an understanding of what is being asked. Sometimes it doesn't take much time for what seems like a large project, or vice versa.

Concentrate on one goal at a time: How do you determine what matters? How do you determine what is essential for your organization? Is it the use of key performance indicators? Well, whatever the priority of your business is, executing is your task. One way is through the Ninety-Ninety-One rule to do this. If you manage a team, it also works.

As suggested by HR guru Robin Sharma "Here's what you do: commit to the most important task for the first ninety minutes of your day for ninety days. With this method, your priorities will be focused on before the day really gets going.

It's very practical as well. It's not spending your entire time on a single thing every day.

You can also set up initiatives to concentrate on this one objective and ensure it aligns with the general objectives of your business.

Track your time for patterns to be identified: Tracking your time, even if no one asks you for it, can assist you in knowing your working practices and the time of day when you most effectively complete your job. Effectively tracking your time and knowing what your tech habits are, from checking your email to checking how often your favorite websites or social media, can have a large impact on your working day.

Keeping track of your time for one or two weeks will assist you in seeing where you're spending your time and assist you in better estimating your objectives, subsequently.

You will also notice areas where you tend to be less productive or recognize some planning mistakes you can work around— such as weekly conferences or appointments.

Share tasks and follow-up: Giving your team duties and projects is one thing; making sure they complete the job and get it done is another thing. Then passing it on for approvals is another piece of the pie you've got to deal with. It will make your job more effective by finding a reliable technique to track the projects of your team. Collaboration tools and project management software can definitely help with this (more on this later), but you must also commit to using tools like this so that you don't let your colleagues down. But also in this, your personal aspect is essential.

Creating a proactive dashboard: I stole this concept from App Sumo's founder, Noah Kagan. This is essentially a measurable list of tasks. If you notice that a certain assignment has a large impact on what you do, then list the number of things you need to do to carry out the task every week. However, the goal here is to record inputs, not just results.

This is particularly helpful to marketers. If you understand that you need to tweet or write a number of LinkedIn posts, you can post them and make sure you do that amount for the week. Here's a proactive dashboard instance:

Figure Your Two Peak Hours: Some of us are morning persons, and some are owls of the night. But this is not always accommodated by the contemporary company setting. The office may not be open until 9 o'clock, but your peak is between 5 am and 7 am. I consider myself a morning person and I personally find performing duties in the early hours of the day to be less tiresome. Often, I will deliberately spend some time at that moment or plan more less-strategic duties in hours when I'm not as tired. It is suggested that we should find at least two hours a day to dive into the more difficult strategic job and leave the other hours for conferences or less urgent assignments.

You will also recognize patterns, and then for longer periods of time, you can participate in a "profound job" or the concept of a centered job. This is the idea of Professor Cal Newport from

Georgetown. Some work (such as answering messages) is shallow, while others (such as fresh campaign ideas or intense photo editing) may require more concentrated time or "profound work."

Declutter: Do you know that your job affects your physical environment? And I don't just mean if you're working or not in a "cool" office. It's mainly out of your control, depending on your business and your position in the company. But your workspace can be controlled. If you don't have to chase and peck for anything that's missing, it enables you to be more productive. By not doing that, you will save time. For your duties at hand, you will also get more clarity and concentration. Check here for more advice.

Find time to work out: During my clinical rotations in graduate school, I'd make a conscious effort to walk on the treadmill for at least 30 minutes at the local gym.

It's not about keeping fit or losing weight, but practice can assist you in making yourself more productive as it improves your alertness. Because it improves your blood flow and cardiovascular health, you are going to be less nervous, more concentrated, and more able to cope with stress.

Stop and think: If you are the type that is not always productive, you need to reflect and see what works, what isn't, what needs to be prioritized and what needs to be changed. Building time to review is not a waste of time, but it optimizes your productivity.

Ask for assistance on things you don't know: If you're proud (like me!), you don't like to ask for assistance on stuff you feel like you can do. This manifests in my life by taking too long to format an Excel sheet or to produce the ideal presentation of PowerPoint. Instead, clever individuals are asking for assistance. And their peers truly see them as smarter. Not to mention, in the long run, this might save you loads of time. Yes, watching a video or calling a support line may be hard at first to spare a few additional minutes here and there, but in the end, it will assist you to be more effective with these assignments.

CHAPTER SUMMARY

- Being productive is not a sudden decision
- Productivity is achieved by consistency and making positive changes
- Making a to-do list can help to breaking big objectives into smaller ones
- Time tracking and focusing on your goals are important ways you can be productive

ACTION PLANS

1. As of now, I will embrace productivity while working toward my goals.

2. As of now, I will _____

_____

_____

_____

_____

_____

_____

_____

_____

_____

_____

_____

_____

IN DUE TIME

"Hold on to your dreams of a better life and stay committed to striving to realize it."

—EARL G. GRAVES SR.

CHAPTER 12

ADDITIONAL MASTERPIECE PRINCIPLES

There are many other principles that need to be followed if you want to achieve your goals.

I will be talking about those points below.

Mastermind alliance

Every affluent person I researched relied on a small, tight-knit group of people who understood their passion for their main purpose or objective. Not Jesus, but the disciples who had a single goal were what made Jesus the greatest and most effective preacher of all time. I don't think anyone would be familiar with Jesus now if not for his disciples. Wealthy people are all too aware of this. They surround themselves with a mastermind alliance or brain trust whose very existence is to carry out their primary objective or goal. No big goal can be accomplished without a mastermind alliance; we are only as great as the people we surround ourselves with.

You need to surround yourself with a group of people who share your passion for your major goal in life if you want to succeed in fulfilling it. The core team of advisors that Andrew Carnegie referred to was his mastermind alliance. He never took any action without first consulting them. Each decision he took was discussed with his inner circle. You need disciples if you want to fulfill your main goal.

Fanaticism

With regard to their main goal, wealthy people are fanatics. Every day they live, breathe and eat in the service of their goal. Their brain trust lives and breathes their mission every day. You and your group need to be equally fanatical for a crucial reason. The followers of Jesus, the inner circle of Andrew Carnegie, Bill Gates, and Steven Jobs were all fervent believers. Pulling the cart becomes a lot simpler when you and your crew have a maniacal fixation on reaching a shared goal. No wealthy person can push the cart by themselves.

To achieve the main objective or goal, they require a fervent group of disciples.

Fanatical followers will appear out of nowhere to assist you in achieving your mission or goal once you discover your core objective. The best sign that you have really discovered your main mission in life is that. Find something you are truly passionate about, make it your life's purpose, share it with others, choose your fervent followers, and then pursue your life's purpose as a group with fervor.

Enjoy the process

The adage "It's not whether you win or lose; it's how you play the game" is common knowledge. The same is true for developing and achieving goals; regardless of the outcome, take pleasure in the journey. Think about it…

You decide to achieve a long-term objective in two years. You keep doing everything you can to position yourself for timely completion of the goal during the course of the two years. You put in a lot of effort, and after two years, you succeed in achieving your objective. However, you then realize that you wasted two years of your life, not enjoying the journey to get there.

Despite the fact that this is true, you might not be joyful due to the unhappiness you forced upon yourself over the course of those two years. Even though you've accomplished your goal, you realize how quickly the last few years have passed, and you start to doubt whether the two years were worthwhile.

Start appreciating the process that you must go through in order to finally obtain the end result if you want to make sure that a two-year goal (or a goal of any other period of time) will be worthwhile. The more you appreciate it, the more you'll want to keep working toward that objective. One of the most valuable resources available to man is time.

ADDITIONAL MASTERPIECE PRINCIPLES

If you give up a considerable portion of your time with the sole intention of achieving your goal, you can find yourself feeling pretty disappointed that your life has been consumed by the pursuit of that objective. Because of this, it's important to choose meaningful goals that bring you joy while pursuing your desired results.

You will become adept at continually following the proper path to success as soon as you begin adhering to these rules! Life aspiration should come naturally to those who aim high. Instead of continuing to live your existing life of predictable outcomes, strive to improve and apply this advice to help you become and remain successful.

Reward yourself for your progress

Create mini-milestones on the path to your objective, and give yourself rewards when you reach them. You might be imagining that if you lose 50 pounds, you'll think of a treat to give yourself after you hit the milestones of 10 pounds lost, 25 pounds lost, and 40 pounds lost.

Three benefits will result from achieving these milestones:
1. The reward will spur you on to work more and accomplish the final objective.
2. You'll see that you're progressing well in completing these milestones.
3. You'll be able to track your progress and estimate how long it will take to complete the goal in its entirety or to reach your next milestone.

It's a good idea to set smaller goals to help you succeed since, frequently, people lose sight of their vision when they consider how enormous their goal or desire is and contrast it with their actual situation. Success means making steady progress toward your objective; if you give up, you won't be successful.

Track your results

People are highly motivated by results. They base their assessments of their life on the outcomes they are experiencing, and these outcomes can either spur them on or sap their drive to pursue a particular objective. People are more driven to keep working to produce greater results, the more results they see heading in a positive way. If at all feasible, record your findings and keep track of them. For whatever your aim is, frequently review your data so you can monitor the progress you're making. (Keep in mind that every objective should be measurable to allow you to monitor your progress.)

Realize the "Why"

Why do you want to be fit? Why do you want to lose some pounds? Why do you want to have a change in career? The WHYs are very important because, in your darkest moment, they keep you going. The answers should be your driving force.

If your Whys and the answers aren't solid enough, then you will be easily demotivated. It is funny, but even the silliest "Why" could be a pushing force. Let's say you want to lose some pounds to shame an ex who didn't love you because of your size. So, you hit the gym daily with such ferocity that people watch you in awe. You do this because you want to look attractive at that party. Yes, you do make an entrance at the party, turning heads. And yes, you love that surprised look on your ex's face. But you know what could be even better? Being fit for yourself!

Having an external reason, such as validation from others, for your Whys tends to last short-term and may not turn out the way we want. That ex from your past might not even care. They might be married to an attractive woman or man, and you may end up being hurt, with another goal to lose some pounds in order to look like their spouse.

Losing weight for me was something I did that was personal to me and my future. My mother would often tell me a story of how I cried when I was younger about not wanting to become old. Years later, I realized my concern with aging was actually about being crippled by diseases such as diabetes, cancer, and high blood pressure. So whenever I feel like quitting, I always refer back to my Whys. The answers resonated deeply in me and kept me going.

Understand your Whys and hold on to them. The days that you feel like giving up, they will motivate you to keep on going.

A goal usually has motivational factors behind it that help us succeed. Realizing why you want the goal could be all that is necessary; this is a significant issue, so don't ignore it. In fact, you should list at least 5 reasons why you want your objective when you are setting it. These motivating factors will help you achieve your objective. When that moment arrives, and you do achieve your goal, they will also develop the justification for why you will be content. The motivation behind a goal will help you get through the challenging moments and inspire persistence to ultimately succeed.

Create an incentive for reaching your goals

Other than considering whys, you might also come up with tangible rewards for accomplishing your goal.

I once read in a fitness book that someone intended to "run" the distance between Geographical Point A to Point B. They would not physically run from city to city but would run the equivalent distance through exercise in X amount of time. For example, let's say someone wanted to run from New York to L.A. over the course of two years using an elliptical or treadmill. For motivational purposes, they'd donate $500 to a buddy to keep in order to increase the incentive for them to maintain their fitness routine and to make sure they would eventually achieve their objective. They would receive their money back and be free to utilize it however they see fit once they achieve their goal (which they did). The money would be given to a certain charity that the runner predetermined in advance if they didn't reach their objective by the finish date.

If you establish additional motivation for yourself to accomplish the goal beyond just the objective itself, this will assist in keeping you moving consistently on the path of success and achievement.

Never quit

Even if successful people make mistakes and encounter failure, they never make excuses and never give up. The statement that "many of life's failures are people who did not recognize how near they were to success when they quit up" was made by Thomas Edison, of all people, and is absolutely accurate. Only with constant daily effort and work over an extended period of time over many years are goals and desires realized, success is attained, and our entire potential is realized. No matter what happens along the way, resolve right now that you will never give up and keep trying until you succeed.

You can become and do anything, and the formula above is the secret to realizing your life's ambitions. But in order to achieve your goals, you need to take care that your life's top objectives are not threatened and that you develop the traits that are essential for real success. Real success in life is decided by who we ultimately become, the qualities we cultivate, and the people we support along the road. It is not always about achieving the goal or desire.

Developing a character of integrity, values, and unselfishness is why we are here, and fortunately, when these same qualities are combined with the laws of success, we will achieve our goals and dreams and experience true success in life. We need to give when we receive, put God and family first, and recognize that these are the reasons we are here.

CHAPTER SUMMARY

- When you start a journey of success, never quit until you reach the destination
- Even if people don't praise you for what you do, praise yourself
- Always have a solid reason why you want to do something

FINAL NOTE

I will also use this medium to urge you to learn from this book. You can do this by reading and reading again as you will understand all the lessons word for word. When you learn from the lessons, have a plan to put them into practice. Because research has shown that there are many things we have learned in life that we never try to practice.

The beauty of whatever you learn in life is to practice it so that you will be the one to benefit from the outcome.

Thanks for reading – go and make those lessons work for you.

Keep winning.

Made in the USA
Columbia, SC
20 September 2022

67656579R00076